Mobile Days

By Andrew Einspruch

Harcourt Achieve
Rigby • Saxon • Steck-Vaughn

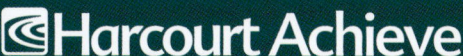

www.HarcourtAchieve.com
1.800.531.5015

PM Extensions Nonfiction
Sapphire

U.S. Edition © 2013 HMH Supplemental Publishers
10801 N. MoPac Expressway
Building #3
Austin, TX 78759
www.hmhsupplemental.com

Text © 2005 Cengage Learning Australia Pty Limited
Illustrations © 2005 Cengage Learning Australia Pty Limited
Originally published in Australia by Cengage Learning Australia

All rights reserved. No part of this work may be reproduced or transmitted in any form or by any means, electronic or mechanical, including photocopying or recording, or by any information storage and retrieval system, without the prior written permission of the copyright owner unless such copying is expressly permitted by federal copyright law. Requests for permission to make copies of any part of the work should be addressed to Houghton Mifflin Harcourt Publishing Company, Attn: Contracts, Copyrights, and Licensing, 9400 Southpark Center Loop, Orlando, Florida 32819.

4 5 6 7 8 9   1957   14
19255

Text: Andrew Einspruch
Printed in China by 1010 Printing International Ltd

Mobile Days
ISBN 978 0 75 789264 6

Contents

A mobile world:	4
Nomads—the first mobile people	6
Trains made the world smaller	8
And then came the car	10
Human turtles	12
Faster and faster, farther and farther	14
Mobile profile: **Standing scooter**—*the future of mobility?*	16
Motion is not activity	18
Don't worry, we'll come to you	20
Mobile profile: **Air Ambulance Rescue**	22
Things on the move	24
Mobile profile: **Portable computers**	26
So is all this moving around a good idea?	28
Moving into the future	30
Glossary	32
Index	32

A mobile world

Have you ever ridden in a car? Flown in a plane? Talked on a cell phone? Used a laptop computer? Listened to a personal stereo?

Has your family ever driven across town or to another city just to visit a relative or friend for the day?

Perhaps you have lived in more than one place during your life. Maybe you changed cities, states, or even countries.

If you have done any of these things, you definitely belong to our modern, mobile world.

The development of cars and planes in the 20th century meant people were more mobile than ever before.

What is "mobile"?

If something is *mobile*, it can move around. It can become mobile on its own power or by someone or something carrying it.

A jellyfish is mobile—it moves in the water. A cell phone is mobile—you can take it with you. A skyscraper is not mobile—it stays in one place.

When we talk about people being mobile, we mean that they can move from place to place easily. They may travel short distances (such as to the store) or long distances (such as across the planet).

Computers have become small enough to be carried easily.

The invention of personal stereos in the 1970s and 1980s allowed people to listen to music anywhere.

Nomads—
the first mobile people

Some people have lived mobile lives for thousands of years. *Nomads* do not live in any one place. Instead, they spend their lives moving around, following the seasons and looking for food and water.

Kiowa

If nomads are hunters, they might follow animals. For example, the Kiowa are Native Americans who live in an area called the Great Plains. Until around 150 years ago, they moved with the buffalo herds, which they hunted and used for food, clothing, and shelter.

The Kiowa made cone-shaped tents, called *tepees*, from buffalo skins and wooden poles. These were easy to pack and move. When the Kiowa traveled, they carried items in a *travois*, which was a kind of sling made from skins, and tepee poles that were pulled by a horse or dog.

Native Americans lived in tepees, which were easy to move.

The Kiowa hunted buffalo.

Bedouin

If nomads are herders, they might move around looking for places where their stock can eat. For example, Bedouin tribes in the Middle East travel between grazing lands and water holes in and around the desert with their camels. Some Bedouin tribes herd goats, sheep, or cattle. Bedouin live in tents made of camel or goat hair.

Around 10 percent of people in the Middle East are still nomadic Bedouins. However, the life is very difficult, and there is always pressure from governments and city dwellers for them to settle in one place.

These modern-day Bedouins herd sheep.

This map shows where modern-day Bedouins live.

Trains made the world smaller

Two hundred years ago, if you weren't a nomad, you probably didn't move around much. Before the 1800s, people rarely went more than 18 miles from home because it took too long to travel.

Some people rode horses or sailed ships. However most people could not afford to travel that way, so they walked or stayed home.

And then came trains.

Steam-powered trains were invented in England around 1800, and quickly spread across that country and around the world.

Suddenly people traveled much farther and more often than ever before. By the late 1800s, trains could move at 60 miles an hour, which meant you could go further in 20 minutes than most people had previously traveled in a lifetime.

Trains made distances appear to shrink. A destination that once took days to reach by horse-drawn carriage was a few comfortable hours away by train.

This had a huge effect on people's lives. People saw places and things they would never have seen before. Their choices of what they could see and do, and more importantly, with whom they could travel, exploded beyond the boundaries of their town or village. Travel gave them the chance to meet many more people.

The train, like nothing before it, got everyone moving and was the start of the mobile world.

Think about this

How were the changes caused by planes and air travel similar to changes caused by trains?

And then came the car

If trains got people moving, the car changed *everything* about life—where people lived, where they worked, whom they knew, and where they could go. Having a car meant freedom.

The problem with trains was they only went to certain places at specific times. But with a car, you could go anywhere you wanted when it suited you.

Despite early developments in Europe, it was the United States that gave the car to the world. In the early 1900s, cars began to be mass-produced in factories, which enabled them to be made and sold cheaply. This meant lots of people could afford them. Americans bought cars by the thousands, and the rest of the world was close behind.

The Model T Ford was one of the first affordable cars.

Like the train, the car had an enormous impact. What started as a luxury soon became a necessity. People came to depend on the car for their social life, for getting them to work and school, and for shopping. For people living in the country, having a car meant the end of **isolation**, because neighbors and towns were suddenly easy to get to.

If it weren't for cars, there would be no suburbs, shopping malls, drive-through fast-food shops, or motels, and no need for highways.

Try this

Keep a list of everywhere you go in the car for four days, including a weekend. Now imagine what it would be like if you could only walk or ride a horse.

Modern shopping centers have huge parking lots.

Human turtles

What happens when you add wheels to a house? You end up with a mobile home or trailer. With one of these, you can move your whole life around.

People liked the idea of taking their things with them when they traveled by car. A mobile home or trailer let them keep at least part of home close by.

The idea of taking home with you is not new. Nomads have been doing it for thousands of years. Gypsy caravans pulled by horses have been used for 500 years. However having a car meant you could take more things than a horse could pull, and you could travel farther and faster with it.

A brightly decorated gypsy caravan

Trailers, which are pulled by cars, first appeared in the United States in 1926. They were used as a home away from home when people went camping. Later, when American soldiers returned from World War II, they often had trouble finding a place to live. The solution was often a mobile home, which was **affordable** and let the soldier move his family to places where there were jobs.

An early trailer

A modern trailer

Today thousands of people roam the world, some **permanently** and some just on vacation, pulling a home behind their car.

Did you know?

Around 50 million motor vehicles are made every year.

Faster and faster, farther and farther

Planes, trains, and cars let people move faster and farther. However it seems as if people always want to go that little bit faster or that little bit farther.

Die Autobahn

Germany has a highway system called the *Autobahn* where, on about half of it, you are allowed to drive as fast as you safely can. There's a suggested limit of 80 miles an hour, but it's only a suggestion. The average speed on some parts is 90 to 100 miles an hour, and some people drive at over 125 miles an hour.

Bullet trains

In the 1960s, Japanese bullet trains sped along at 125 miles an hour. Today they rocket along at speeds of more than 185 miles an hour.

Faster than sound

People seem to want to fly faster, too. The world's only commercial **supersonic** jet, the Concorde, flew from 1976 to 2003 at twice the **speed of sound**, or 1,367 miles an hour. It carried 2.5 million passengers on 50,000 flights. Where a normal jet takes seven to eight hours to get from London to New York, the Concorde did it in three-and-a-half hours.

The Concorde flew at twice the speed of sound.

Who needs to go that fast?

Being able to move quickly means you spend less time traveling and more time working or having fun when you get there. If a businessperson could save four-and-a-half hours by flying on the Concorde, then there was that much more time for meetings.

The bullet train means Japanese people can live farther away from work, but still get there in a reasonable amount of time.

Many Japanese people travel to work on the bullet train.

Highways allow more cars to go fast at the same time without having to stop.

Did you know?

There is no speed limit on some rural highways. But you still have to drive safely.

15

Mobile profile:

Standing scooter—
the future of mobility?

A standing scooter, introduced in 2001, is a self-balancing, motorized, electric scooter that looks like a pair of wheels with a stick and a handle. Turn it on and you have the latest in personal transportation. To go, you simply lean forward. To stop or go backwards, lean back. You turn right or left by turning the handlebar.

A standing scooter takes up about the same space as an adult **pedestrian**. It has a top speed of 12 miles an hour and can go where any human can walk. It is perfect for zipping around the city as well as indoors.

What's really interesting is that it keeps balance for you. A standing scooter has five **gyroscopes** (also found in ships, planes, and missiles) that sense even the smallest movements. The unit constantly adjusts in order to stay under you and keep upright.

This is more than a bike or scooter. The machine is balanced whether it is standing still or moving, and it provides the power, not you. There are two electric motors for each wheel, and a standing scooter does not cause air pollution.

A standing scooter may well be how we all get from here to there in the future.

A standing scooter can go anywhere a person can walk.

Motion is not activity

Just because we have become more mobile doesn't mean we're better off in all ways.

With so many forms of transportation, we have lots of choices about how to get from here to there. One form of transportation that people are using less and less frequently is the one they used to use more than any other—their bodies.

Even though in our mobile world we're moving more than ever, people are becoming less and less active. The result is that, in Western society, people are getting bigger and bigger.

This isn't good. Obesity (being overweight) is unhealthy and can lead to lots of diseases and even early death. The more conveniences we add to our lives, the less our bodies have to do, and the harder it is to stay in shape.

People are spending more time watching TV, which does not burn much energy.

Think about it. Three hundred years ago, if you wanted to get somewhere, you probably walked. Walking burned energy. Also, life back then involved a lot of physical work because most people were farmers.

When you ride in a car today, you don't burn much energy at all. Even simple things, like standing up to change the channel on the TV, have been replaced by remote controls and other gadgets.

So the more mobile we become, the more work we have to do to stay healthy. Next time you have to go somewhere, think about walking.

Playing in a sport is one way of maintaining our health.

Don't worry, we'll come to you

Sometimes it isn't people that are mobile—it's the services that they need.

Learning on wheels

Not everyone can get to a library. Some, like elderly or sick people, find it difficult to leave home. Others live too far away or in communities that are too poor to have a library. In many places, these people can take advantage of mobile libraries that come to them.

Mobile libraries, sometimes called "bookmobiles," are vans or buses that travel around bringing books and information to people. Usually bookmobiles follow a planned route to visit a series of places. They lend library materials, such as books, CDs, audio books, and videos. Some even have Internet connections.

A mobile library in a rural town

The bookmobile stops in each place for a short time (maybe an hour or a day), then returns a week or a month later to collect loaned material and lend new items.

Inside a mobile library

Mobile libraries don't have to be vans or buses. In some countries trains, boats, and even camels are used to bring learning materials to people.

In Kenya, Africa, camels are used to carry books to primary schools.

Mobile profile:
Air Ambulance Rescue

Air ambulance rescue is one of the most successful ways to move wounded soldiers from battle. In rural areas, it's a common way to move people who need urgent medical attention to big hospitals.

Orville and Wilbur Wright flew the world's first airplane in 1904. Rescuing people by airplane began soon after. During World War I, the U.S. Army needed to rescue more wounded soldiers faster. By 1918, Major Nelson E. Driver and Captain William C. Ocker adapted the design of the rear cockpit

in their JN-4 "Jenny" biplane to become an open space for one injured soldier. Biplane air ambulances made the impossible possible. Even with this success, medical flights were highly dangerous. With each failure, engineers saw new ways to improve the next air ambulance. No one was giving up on learning how to air rescue soldiers safely! Between 1943 and 1944 during World War II, the 8th Air Force crew went from rescuing 1.5 to 43 percent of all wounded soldiers. Air rescue has been used in wartime rescue ever since.

Today air ambulance and rescue is an industry that extends far beyond wartime needs. Tens of thousands of people just like you are rescued by air ambulances. Each year private air ambulance companies, in every state and around the world, fly hundreds of patients to hospitals for urgent medical care.

Things on the move

The more people move around, the more they invent things to take with them.

Want to listen to some music? Plug into your personal stereo. The first ones appeared in 1979 and played cassette tapes. Then came small units in the 1980s and 1990s that played CDs. They were followed by today's models that play music downloaded from the Internet.

A personal CD player

This machine plays music downloaded from the Internet.

Need to make a phone call? No problem. It seems as if almost everyone has a mobile phone these days.

Mobile phones mounted in cars date back as far as 1924. Car telephones became common in the early 1980s, and heavy **portable** phones appeared around the same time. By the late 1980s, phones had shrunk to a convenient size. During the 1990s, they became even smaller and more popular.

A car phone in 1959

Technology blending

As our mobile gadgets get smaller, they also seem to overlap. Your mobile phone may have a radio or a camera in it or connect to the Internet. Your hand-held computer may include a phone.

People like the functions they can get from these items, but they still want them to be convenient. Otherwise they'll get left at home.

Mobile profile:
Portable computers

Electronic computers have only been around since World War II, and personal computers first appeared in the late 1970s. It wasn't long after that when someone started thinking, "Hey, if I could carry one of these things around, I could work wherever I want to."

That gave us the portable computer.

One of the first portable computers appeared in 1981. At 22 pounds, it was quite heavy, and did not have a battery, so you had to plug it in. It had a tiny screen and used two $5\frac{1}{4}$-inch floppy drives for storage. Still it could do word processing, spreadsheets, and database work.

One of the first portable computers, in 1983

The first real laptop computer appeared in 1987. It had a flip-up screen in the lid, which closed down over the keyboard. It weighed around 7 pounds.

Today's notebooks

Companies kept making laptops smaller, lighter, more powerful, and with better batteries. People started calling them *notebooks* because they were about the size of one. They eventually came with color screens, modems, built-in pointers, CD-ROMs, and DVDs.

Portable computers mean that you can take your work with you wherever you go.

So is all this moving around a good idea?

We can go more places, meet more people, and do more things than ever before. From cars to planes, phones to computers, our lives seem to get faster and busier every day.

There's always a cost, and that's something you need to think about. The freedom a car gives us means we have more choices, and the ability to choose more things. We have to make sure those are good choices for us. It's great to be able to phone someone from the middle of a baseball stadium or the top of a skyscraper, but are we better off for it? Couldn't we use the nearest pay phone?

With all of the technological change, bad comes with the good. Cars, planes, buses, and trains all bring mobility, but they also create noise, traffic and pollution.

Cell phones give us the chance to be constantly in touch with friends and family. They are equally annoying when they go off in restaurants or at the movies.

Combine a hand-held phone and a car driver, and you have a recipe for an accident.

The world, having become mobile, has changed forever, and will keep on changing. It is up to all of us to make sure the changes are good ones.

Moving into the future

If people continue becoming more and more mobile, what will the future look like?

Perhaps we will have cars that drive themselves, leaving us to read or work while we travel. Maybe we'll have eyeglasses that have a radio, cell phone, and Internet connection all built in.

Perhaps we will become mobile enough to go to other planets, the way we can now go to other countries. Imagine a vacation in space—on the Moon, or on Mars? It might just happen in your lifetime.

Who knows what the future holds? Whatever happens one thing is almost certain—we will continue to stay on the move.

Glossary

affordable — able to be bought fairly inexpensive

gyroscope — a spinning wheel mounted in one or more rings on a base that can stay upright even if its base moves

isolation — not having much contact with other people

pedestrian — a person who is walking

permanently — for all time

portable — able to be moved or carried easily

speed of sound — the speed at which sound waves travel through the air

supersonic — faster than the speed of sound

wireless — a radio receiver

Index

air ambulance   22–23
Autobahn   14

Bedouins   7
bookmobiles   20–21
bullet trains   14–15

caravans   12
cars   4, 10–14, 19, 28, 31
cell phones   4–5, 24, 28, 31
computers   4, 25–28
Concorde   14

Internet   20, 24–25, 31

Kiowa   6

laptop computers   4, 27

mobile homes   12, 13
mobile libraries   20–21

nomads   6–8, 12

obesity   18

personal stereos   4, 24
planes   4, 9, 14, 22, 28
pollution   28
portable computers   26–27

standing scooter   16–17

trailers   13
trains   8–11, 14–15, 28